Taking Charge of Quality

T0129466

Taking Charge of Quality

How Teachers and Unions Can Revitalize Schools

An Introduction and Companion to
United Mind Workers

Charles Taylor Kerchner,
Julia E. Koppich & Joseph G. Weeres

Jossey-Bass Publishers • San Francisco

Copyright © 1998 by Jossey-Bass Inc., Publishers, 350 Sansome Street, San Francisco, California 94104.

All rights reserved. No part of this publication may be reproduced, stored in a retrieval system, or transmitted, in any form or by any means, electronic, mechanical, photocopying, recording, or otherwise, without the prior written permission of the publisher.

Interior design by Bruce Lundquist

Jossey-Bass books and products are available through most bookstores. To contact Jossey-Bass directly, call (888) 378-2537, fax to (800) 605-2665, or visit our website at www.josseybass.com.

Substantial discounts on bulk quantities of Jossey-Bass books are available to corporations, professional associations, and other organizations. For details and discount information, contact the special sales department at Jossey-Bass.

For sales outside the United States, please contact your local Simon & Schuster International Office.

Library of Congress Cataloging-in-Publication Data
Kerchner, Charles T.
    Taking charge of quality : how teachers and unions can revitalize schools : an introduction and companion to United mind workers / Charles Taylor Kerchner, Julia E. Koppich & Joseph G. Weeres. — 1st ed.
        p. cm.
    Includes bibliographical references.

    ISBN 0–7879–4334–7 (pbk.)
    1. Teachers' unions—United States. 2. Collective bargaining—Teachers—United States. 3. Teachers—United States. 4. Educational change—United States. I. Koppich, Julia. II. Weeres, Joseph G., date. III. Kerchner, Charles T. United mind workers. IV. Title.
LB2844.53.U6 K473 1998
331.88'113711'00973—ddc21   98–8952

FIRST EDITION
        10 9 8 7 6 5 4 3 2 1

Contents

Introduction   1

Part I: A Call to Action   3

  1. The Educational Challenges   5

  2. What Can Teachers and Unions Do?   11

Part II: A Commitment to Quality   17

  3. Improving the Craft of Teaching   19

  4. Upgrading Educational Standards   26

  5. Evaluating the Work of Peers   32

Part III: Organizing Around Transforming
   Schools   39

  6. New Contracting Strategies   41

  7. Hiring and Rewarding Teachers   49

  8. Creating More Career Flexibility
   for Teachers   52

  9. What Teachers Can Do Now   58

Conclusion: Organizing the Other Half
   of Teaching   61

Resources   62

Organizations   63

The Authors   64

Introduction

THE WRITING IS ON THE WALL: American education is going to change. As we enter the twenty-first century, the way we educate children will need to undergo profound transformation so our students will be prepared for the world they are going to enter, a world where knowledge, not industry, is the organizing principle.

Taking Charge of Quality argues that teachers and teacher unions should take the lead in these changes. While unions have succeeded admirably in organizing teachers' economic rights, they have left the major decisions about education to management. We believe that teachers are our nation's "mind workers"—the people who know best about teaching and learning. It is they who need to take charge of improving education.

We make this case in *United Mind Workers: Unions and Teaching in the Knowledge Society*. *Taking Charge of Quality* aims to make the issues raised in *United Mind Workers* available for audiences who are most actively involved in education. It both condenses and expands on *United Mind Workers*, reducing the original book to its essential argument, then adding action points for those involved in the process of educational change.

Who Can Benefit From This Booklet?

Taking Charge of Quality is meant to inspire discussion among a variety of players in the educational arena:

- *Forward-thinking unionists* will find *Taking Charge of Quality* essential reading as they address the role of unionism in the knowledge age.

- *Education policymakers* will want to consider its questions as they set the agenda for education reform.

- *Practitioners*—including teachers and administrators—can use *Taking Charge of Quality* to connect their daily experiences in schools to the larger societal context in which they operate.

Organization of This Booklet

Taking Charge of Quality is divided into three parts. Part I describes how American society is changing and how these shifts necessitate the transformation of American education. Part II explores the role we believe teachers and unions must take in bringing about educational change. And Part III lays out our proposal for how unions can organize around a primary commitment to improving education.

Each chapter in *Taking Charge of Quality* presents material from *United Mind Workers* and then asks what teachers and unions can do now about the issues raised. At the conclusion of each chapter are suggestions for "Taking Charge in Thought and Action."

Taking Charge of Quality is a user-friendly, action-oriented booklet. Readers who want to pursue any of the areas addressed here in more depth can look at *United Mind Workers* or on our web site: www.cgu.edu (click Faculty, Kerchner).

Part I

A Call to Action

AMERICAN PUBLIC SCHOOLS are being asked to do something they have never done before and for which they were not designed: They are being asked to educate the great majority of students to very high academic standards and to prepare them for a world in which "thinking for a living" is the norm, not the exception. As this requirement plays out politically, the winds of change buffet public education—not just individual schools, but the institution as a whole. While these winds blow in many different directions, they strike teaching with a singular force: lots of people on the outside try to tell teachers and school administrators on the inside how to do their work. Some of these outsiders are more or less supportive school reformers; others are entrepreneurs who believe they have found better ways to organize schools and make money at the same time.

No matter who the critics are, the message is the same: public education must change. This is the focus of Part I, in which we look at how the pressure to change creates both a crisis and an opportunity for teachers and other educators. To address the transformation of American schools both as it is happening now and as we believe it will unfold over the next twenty-five years, we

- Identify the criticism and pressure public schools are facing

- Describe how societal changes necessitate changes in education
- Question what teachers and unions can and should do about these pressures ▶

1

The Educational Challenges

EDUCATION CHANGES when society changes. In the late nineteenth century, Americans restructured education to meet the needs of an urbanizing, industrializing society. Now, at the close of the twentieth century, Americans must again restructure education to meet the needs of a new society organized around knowledge.

The Pressure on Public Schools

Many Americans are unhappy with the shape of education in this country. The proliferation of education reform projects reveals widespread public dissatisfaction. The New Standards Project, the Coalition of Essential Schools, the National Board for Professional Teaching Standards, and the standards projects of the different educational disciplines all point to the desire and need for change.

The 1983 publication of *A Nation at Risk* voiced this dissatisfaction most clearly. Educational analyst Paul Cooperman set the tone by proclaiming "Each generation of Americans has outstripped its parents in education, in literacy, and in economic attainment. For the first time in the history of the country, the educational skills of one generation will not surpass, will not equal, will not even approach, those of their parents" (National Commission on Excellence in Education, 1983, p. 9).

But *A Nation at Risk* exaggerated the academic performance problems of public education. The longer one looks, the more difficult it is to find the great decline Cooperman described. Consider the following:

- *Although SAT scores fell in the early 1970s, much of their decline may be attributed to changes in the pool of test takers.* Students who would not have taken the SAT in the past are taking it now; the larger number of test takers may be responsible for drops in scores.

- *The reading and math achievement of virtually all groups monitored by the National Center for Education Statistics have not shown net declines over the past two decades.* Scores for African American and Latino students have actually improved, though they still remain substantially below those of white students.

- *In 1993, the National Assessment of Educational Progress (NAEP) announced that three-fourths of twelfth graders had met the very lofty standards laid out in the early part of the century.* They were able to "develop interpretations from a variety of texts," "understand overall arguments," "recognize explicit aspects of plot and characters," "support global generalizations," "respond personally to texts," and "use major documents to solve real-world problems" (Myers, 1996, p. 1).

Why then so much handwringing about the state of public education? On one level it is because even as schools are improving, public expectations are rising. The better we educate our children, the higher we raise the bar. But there's a more important reason for dissatisfaction: we are educating our students for an industrial society that doesn't exist any more. It's not that students aren't well-educated, as many critics would like to proclaim; it's that they're not appropriately educated for the world they're going to enter.

Societal Change, Educational Change

America is currently in the throes of a profound transformation. For the past century, our society has been built on an industrial foundation. We call it a foundation because it defined not only how goods were produced, but how all of society's major institutions—work and play, city and country, family, and, of course, education—took shape. But as we approach the twenty-first century, our foundation is changing. Industry no longer gives form to our lives as it once did. Instead knowledge is the organizing principle of modern society. In the new order, knowledge joins the traditional trio of labor, land, and capital as a source of wealth and power. As industry shaped society's institutions in the past, knowledge will shape them in the future.

The assumptions of the knowledge era are very different from those of the industrial era that preceded it, as the following chart shows.

Industrial Era	Knowledge Era
■ Organization by scale: bigger is better	■ Organization by scope: smaller can be more effective
■ Specialized tasks and workers	■ Flexible tasks and workers
■ Scientific management: clearly-defined tasks enforced by managers	■ Autonomy/self-direction: changing tasks organized and adapted to by workers

Industrial assumptions have shaped education in general—and teachers' work in particular—as much as they have shaped other institutions. We don't mean to suggest that working in a school was like working in a factory. Anyone who has ever worked in a factory knows that's not the case. Nonetheless, industrial assumptions have ruled education and left their imprints on how schools are organized—and how educators' jobs are defined.

Each of the shifting assumptions laid out in the preceding chart plays out generally on a cultural level and specifically in the field of education. Consider the following:

- The idea that bigger was better drove the consolidation of school districts in rural areas and the unification of districts in cities. The number of school districts in the country fell from three hundred thousand to fewer than fifteen thousand today.
  By contrast, schools in the knowledge era will operate more effectively as quasi-independent entities.

- The idea that specialized was efficient gave rise to high school departmentalization and to separate career paths for school administrators and teachers.
  The new era will require more flexibility and mixing of traditional roles by teachers and administrators—as well as students.

- The idea of scientific management gave school administrators the mantle of technical expertise, some freedom from school board domination, and a clearly established organizational superiority over teachers.
  Teachers in the knowledge era—and the students they will prepare for the workforce—will need to be adaptable decision makers operating with greater autonomy.

Perhaps the most striking way in which the industrial paradigm has shaped education involves tracking students. Tracking, which has been a cornerstone of American education in the industrial era, assumes a basic inequality among students that Americans are loathe to admit. In contrast, the knowledge society will require us to educate all students to high standards.

The Industrial Paradigm	The Knowledge Paradigm
■ Not all students are capable of achieving at high levels, a premise that suits an industrial society very well.	■ All students can achieve at high levels, a premise that suits the knowledge society very well.
■ The tracking system produces workers for the large numbers of manufacturing and assembly jobs created by industrialism. Students who did not complete a rigorous high school program still have many opportunities.	■ The new economy demands more and forgives less than its predecessor. It's not creating good jobs for the unskilled, and so the premium placed on educational attainment is increasing.

When we consider it this way, the problem we identified at the beginning of the chapter becomes obvious: Although they were not created to do so, American schools must now educate all students to high levels of achievement.

Conclusions

Because our goals for student learning are changing so dramatically, what we expect of teaching will also have to change. The next chapter addresses the question: What can teachers and unions do to better prepare students for life in the information age?

GETTING STARTED IN THOUGHT AND ACTION

Explore the changes laid out in Chapter 1 with the following thought and action plan.

Thought

▶ Read about the new economy. Books such as Robert Reich's *The Work of Nations* or Richard Murnane and Frank Levy's *The New Basic Skills* provide a readable introduction to the changing economy and society and the implications for teaching. William Julius Wilson's *When Work Disappears* provides a stark look at individual and civic life in urban communities devastated by high unemployment.

Action

▶ Find out what the students who left your school (or your school system) two years ago are doing now. Which are thriving in work, further education, and life in general? Which are not? What's the relationship between the school experiences these students had and the lives they are leading?

2

What Can Teachers and Unions Do?

UNTIL RECENTLY, teacher unions have focused almost exclusively on conventional job rights and protection issues—ensuring job security and adequate wages, benefits, and working conditions. They have excelled in that arena. As industrial-style unions, they have provided teachers with the kinds of benefits they have needed as workers.

However, because we're no longer living in an industrial society, the unions' agenda is called to change. We can no longer think of teachers as assembly-line workers who pour knowledge into the heads of students riding by on the educational conveyer belt. Instead we must recognize that teachers are experts in knowledge, craftspeople of the new era, with essential expertise in teaching and learning. Unions must take the lead in transforming education. They must reclaim teaching and learning for teachers, who are, after all, experts in these areas. "United Mind Workers," the title of our book, is more than a play on words; it encapsulates the changing role teachers and teacher unions must take in the knowledge era.

Organizing the Other Half of Teaching

In our view, the primary challenge of today's unions is to construct a successor to the education system of the industrial era. However, reinventing the public education system—building a new institution from the classroom up—will entail a fundamentally different organizing task from the one that unions faced in the 1960s. Industrial-era unions successfully organized the economic rights of teachers by connecting them to collective bargaining and procedural due process; involving teachers in the substance of education—the other half of teaching—remains unorganized.

This task will mean recognizing teachers as knowledge workers—teachers who are empowered with new authority for determining educational policy and practice. The movement to improve educational standards and productivity hinges on efforts to create more autonomous schools that are less subject to bureaucratic controls and more adaptable to innovation. The next step in this movement is to involve teachers more effectively in school-level decision making. Unions can be in the vanguard of this effort.

What Unions Need to Do

To accomplish the new task of unionism, unions will first need to organize around educational quality, around school innovation and productivity, and around career and occupational stability.

- *Defining and measuring quality—for students, for teachers, and for schools—will be a central task for unions.* Teacher credentialing and other standardized procedures are no longer sufficient for ensuring educational quality. Unions need to promote quality in individual outcomes by adhering to high standards in student assessment and in teacher performance review.

- *Unions need to organize around individual schools rather than school districts.* Our strategic reasons for this are the inherent instability of school districts—many of which are changing in scope and function—and the fact that individual schools are the primary locus of educational innovation and productivity. School-based organizing recognizes the new reality of school-based management and meets the need for diversity and efficiency during unsettled times.

- *Unions must focus on building an external labor market for teachers.* Instead of the internal labor market, where job protection rights are linked to particular jobs or districts, our aim is to promote career security for teachers by creating a system of benefit protections and employment support services that would follow a teacher from job to job, in or out of the district. This system would be better suited to changes in the school and district management structures; it also offers teachers greater mobility.

How Unions Need to Change

Taking on this new organizing task will require myriad initiatives to transform both the meaning of teaching and the approach of unions.

- *Unions must enable teachers to take on roles previously left to district administrators: determining schoolwide policies and practices and ensuring the quality of the teaching force in their local schools.* In this way, unions will become a major force in making teaching a true profession.

- *Unions must support teachers in developing their skills and expertise.* Rewarding teachers for improvement will become central to the union's work.

To institute these changes, unions will need to rethink their approach to collective bargaining. Unions' new strategies will need to enhance educational improvement, whereas unions as they are currently constructed may actually limit teacher participation in educational improvement. Consider the following:

- In their current role, unions can offer few incentives for teachers to develop their professional capacity or to improve their classroom teaching practices.
  By contrast, knowledge-era schools, led by knowledge-era unions, will award teachers higher salaries for acquiring new skills and expertise.

- Unions are currently limited in their ability to accommodate changes in school organization and management. Under conventional labor agreements, unions negotiate for an entire district but pay little heed to the needs of individual schools.
  Knowledge-era unions must develop new strategies for ensuring employment security and benefit protections for teachers across schools and districts.

- Most labor agreements actually constrain teacher-management collaboration.
  By contrast, knowledge-era unions must lead the way in school improvement efforts, so that teachers become actively involved in school planning, policymaking, and resource allocation.

Conclusion

When unions change their goals, they will become leaders in educational improvement. Part II lays out what unions can and must do to transform education for the knowledge era.

GETTING STARTED IN THOUGHT AND ACTION

Thought

▶ In your local union, read books about contemporary teaching such as Linda Darling-Hammond's *The Right to Learn* and Deborah Meier's *The Power of Their Ideas.*

Action

▶ Discuss how your local union supports teachers' needs for understanding and influencing the substance of their work, and discuss when the union gets in the way.

Part II

A Commitment to Quality

WITH SOCIETY'S NEEDS and expectations changing dramatically, education is increasingly under fire. Where the industrial teacher union focused on job protection and fair pay, the information age teacher union must engage in efforts to improve the quality of schooling for our students. What shape can these efforts take? That is the focus of Part II.

Teacher unions can embrace three powerful mechanisms for improving the quality of education.

- *Unions must redefine teaching itself.* What should teachers be doing? How can teachers do their jobs better?

- *Unions must create standards for student performance.* What do teachers—the people who work with students every day—think students should know and be able to do? How can participating in setting standards improve both the standards and the strength of the union?

- *Unions must institute peer assistance and review in order to assure quality in classrooms.* When teachers work together, they benefit from each others' experience, and raise the standards of teaching.

Before unions can engage in these three mechanisms for change, however, they must begin with a discussion of the process of learning itself. What creates learning? How can we build schools around it? Only when these questions are answered can teacher unions begin to organize teachers around their essential function—teaching.

Chapter 3 focuses on defining learning and teaching in ways that enhance the performance of both students and teachers. Chapter 4 addresses the need for national standards, and the role of unions in establishing them; and Chapter 5 explores the value of peer review among teachers, and outlines procedures for establishing a peer review system.

In Part II, we

- Define what constitutes learning in the knowledge era
- Define the unions' role in the transformation of teaching
- Explain why unions need to take the lead in establishing educational standards
- Propose a peer review model that would put teachers at the helm in evaluating each others' work ▶

3

Improving the Craft of Teaching

FUNDAMENTAL CHANGE in education begins with changes in the instructional transactions between teachers and students. With society and education in a period of flux, we must ask some fundamental questions that were last considered almost a hundred years ago. We must question our assumptions about who goes to school and for how long, what they study, how they're taught, and what results we expect. The decisions we make will structure classrooms, schools, teaching jobs, and ultimately the way unions represent teachers.

What Constitutes Learning?

As the industrial model has shaped teachers' jobs, it has also shaped beliefs about what constitutes learning. Industrial America organized around the learning psychology of the time, called *behaviorism.* Primarily, individuals were believed to react to external stimuli. This belief brought forth a stimulus-response curriculum that has shaped instruction and school curriculum for nearly a century.

Behaviorist learning theory emphasized teachers arranging and manipulating a student's world to create stimulus-response chains. As Bruer described it, "Teachers would present lessons in small, manageable pieces (stimuli), ask students to give answers (responses), and then dispense reinforcement (preferably positive rather than negative) until their students became conditioned to give the right responses" (Bruer, 1993, p. 8). Students, like Pavlov's dog, could be trained to perform educational feats in the classroom, and later in the work world. Teachers, like Pavlov himself, could provide the training. This view of what constitutes teaching emphasized learning a prescribed curriculum through practice and repetition.

But over the last thirty years this view of what constitutes education has come under scrutiny. No longer subscribing to the notion that student minds are containers waiting to be filled, cognitive psychologists instead developed a model of learning that holds that learners construct frameworks within which they make sense of the world. According to this paradigm, teachers' jobs become helping students develop their minds, rather than simply filling those minds with information.

The following chart identifies the assumptions made about learning under the now outdated industrial-behaviorist model and contrasts these with assumptions based on cognitive theory.

Behaviorist Assumptions:

1 *transferability:* Students automatically transfer learning from one area to another.

2 *passivity:* Learners are essentially passive recipients of knowledge.

Cognitive Assumptions:

1 Students must learn how to transfer learning from one area to another.

2 Learning requires active engagement by students.

3 *conditioning:* Learning is primarily concerned with strengthening stimulus-response bonds.

3 Students need to put the pieces together, and see the big picture, not just the individual parts.

4 *superficiality:* The right answer counts most; short-term task completion takes precedence over in-depth analysis.

4 Looking at underlying problems can lead to longer-term solutions than can looking for a quick fix.

5 *disconnection:* Learning is independent from context.

5 Learning takes place when there are explicit links with "real life" outside school.

Each of these approaches to education suits the society to which it belongs. The behaviorist model trained students to become industrial workers who followed rules and worked on specific, repeated, concrete tasks. The cognitive model, in contrast, trains students to participate in the knowledge society as active, independent-minded problem solvers.

What Constitutes Good Teaching?

Teachers care deeply about children and learning, and they work devilishly hard. Stress and burnout present a serious threat to the teaching corps, and most principals and superintendents put in work weeks that would crush all but the toughest corporate executives, and at a fraction of the pay (Johnson, 1990). Television commentator Robert McNeil had it right when he concluded a program on teaching by saying "No matter who you are, you don't work as hard as . . . teachers."

Yet, despite all the hard work teachers do, education is still in crisis. When people are working hard and the system is not meeting societal expectations, a genuine institutional crisis exists (Walton, 1986). As we discussed in Part I, with society changing so profoundly, current models of teaching and learning no longer fit. Asking teachers to work harder will not produce the results we need, and incremental change is so painfully slow that it loses external support long before it can produce significant results.

What is needed is a profound change in what teachers do every day. In traditional exercises a student can get the so-called right answers by reproducing the examples. We must move away from this to exercises crafted to reveal student thought processes. But this shift requires that teachers encounter great uncertainty—they must follow students' patterns of sense making rather than simply determine the rightness or wrongness of answers. Organizing teaching around understanding, inquiry, and complex problem solving challenges the way teachers teach, the way their jobs are constructed, and the set of work rules surrounding them. When thought of this way, it is clear that changing teaching is inherently union work.

The first struggle that unionized teachers face is the fight against deskilling teaching. Despite all the evidence to the contrary about learning, some legislative and administrative initiatives seek to make teaching more bound by routines and rules about how and when specific instructional techniques are to be used. These initiatives couldn't be more misguided, as virtually every recent instructional improvement shows. Mainstreaming in special education, literature-based curriculum, cross-discipline teaching, theories of multiple intelligences—

all deny the simple classification of students and lead to more complex teaching work.

Unions must take the lead in recognizing and encouraging teacher professionalization. Consider the following realities about teaching in the knowledge era:

- *Teaching in knowledge-era classrooms is less routine because teaching for understanding moves classes away from rote memorization and recitation.* Teaching must encourage active student engagement, which draws on teachers' creativity and their ability to respond to the ever-changing needs of their students.

- *Teaching in knowledge-era classrooms is increasingly personalized and individualized.* Heterogeneous classrooms bring together students with different backgrounds, learning styles, and displayed abilities. In these classrooms, the teacher's job is to make subtle changes in teaching so that students with different attributes can learn in the same physical and social space.

- *Teaching in knowledge-era classrooms involves a broader range of roles.* As industrial specialization has declined, teachers' jobs have expanded. Teachers have been adding counseling, crisis intervention, family mediation, and conflict resolution to their repertoire.

- *Teaching for understanding is less isolated.* While industrial teaching put teachers alone with their students for six hours a day, knowledge-era teachers may work with many more adults: other teachers, parents, social service providers. This interaction helps develop a professional language, but it also punctures the safe, self-made cocoon of individual practice.

- *Teaching must become explicitly connected to knowledge gener-ation.* As the cognitive approach suggests, teaching is about the creation of cognitive constructions in students: it is, quite literally, mind work. Teachers practice their craft daily, but they become professionals only when they reflect on their practice of constructing knowledge.

Conclusions

As teaching is transformed, unions have their work cut out for them facilitating the process of true professionalization for teachers. First, they must insist that teaching be recognized for the increasingly complex job that it is. Second, they must help teachers make the transition from industrial-era practice to knowledge-era practice. Changing schools begins with changing teaching and struggling with the instincts of teachers who believe that the union must protect them to teach as they always have. Finally, unions must make it their business to engage teachers in reflection on what they do every day. Unions need to confront the reality that their purpose is not to make teachers happy in any superficial way. As Meier put it, "What we need is a particular kind of job satisfaction that has as its anchor intellectual growth."

GETTING STARTED IN THOUGHT AND ACTION

Thought

▶ Read about the relationship between teaching and how schools are organized in books such as Susan Moore John-son's *Teachers at Work.*

▶ Read for understanding about the new pedagogies, to be able to distinguish fads from fundamental changes. *United Mind Workers* provides an introduction and references to this literature.

Action

▶ Create a space in school where excellent student work is exhibited, and time when it is talked about.

▶ Develop an understanding of high quality among both teachers and students.

▶ Change conversation in the teachers' room so that student work becomes the focus.

▶ Make school meetings a time to talk about student achievement rather than about announcements and other items that could be handled in other ways.

▶ Organize school so that each student falls within the responsibility of a caring adult.

▶ Develop a teacher role in in-service education and professional development.

4

Upgrading Educational Standards

TEACHERS AND ALL educators can link themselves to quality education by becoming clear and articulate about student standards. Standards establish our expectations for student achievement. Who should be more concerned about defining these expectations than teachers—and their unions? We propose that teachers and teacher unions should be the strongest advocates of educational standards, rather than their avowed enemies.

Aligning teacher unions with the development of standards will require real leadership, for many teachers see national or state standards—and the tests that come with them—as intrusions into their domains and as incomplete indicators of what students know. One finds evidence of this opposition in the ethnographic research on teachers and teaching as well as in the policy positions of teacher unions.

We believe that when unions oppose setting standards, they essentially abdicate responsibility for quality. The NEA's policies in opposition to standardized testing "mandated by local, state, or national authority, and the uses of competency testing" suggest, albeit inadvertently, that the union is not concerned with student achievement. There is, of course, a great deal that is wrong with existing tests, but unions need to be in the forefront of correcting them. A blanket policy of opposition places organized teachers on the wrong side of history.

The Need for Standards

We believe standards are necessary, for reasons that are both idealistic and practical.

Standards define the central mission of education and, in the larger sense, the evolving concept of American nationhood. Standards say what we value; they are an act of civic belief. When we establish standards, we affirm our belief in our educational institutions and in our students. In his 1992 book *Horace's School,* Theodore Sizer noted that the absence of standards reflects badly on Americans' belief in our own democracy:

> Most Americans do not care about rigorous high school education and thoughtlessly accept, for example, the convenience of the massive employment of teenagers on school days and the exquisite entertainment of Friday night football, however it may undermine the players' academic progress. Leaders lie, misuse facts, deliberately distort. The country happily tolerates mediocrity and the conviction that anything which sells must be good. High educational standards are impossible without high civic standards (p. 115).

Enacting standards nationally also makes practical sense because standards serve as a means to regain public confidence in the institution of education. Elementary and secondary education has a credibility problem. The general public doesn't believe that grades and diplomas are good indicators of student achievement. When we set standards and show measurable student attainment to members of the public, they become important allies of the educational system.

In addition, national standards and associated means of assessment can buffer individual schools and their teachers from debilitating local conflicts over the same issues. National standards will help prevent vicious local battles over texts and lessons, fights that should be avoided. Because national organizations can institutionalize standards, local democracies do not have to return to first principles at every Tuesday's school board session.

We're not suggesting that setting educational standards will be easy. We have already seen furious battles over standards—what they are, how to measure them, and how to reflect those measurements in schools. The debates, which have become highly politicized, cut to the core of our educational system. They reflect the need for change, and they speak of our need and desire to educate students for life in the twenty-first century.

No matter how difficult the task, given the importance of educational standards, we believe that unions should take the lead in establishing them. Doing so will position unions as leaders in educational improvement.

- *Test scores are used as indicators of school success or failure.* As the experts in teaching and learning, teachers should be involved in creating these tests. Unions that are involved in creating the tests have a stronger voice in evaluating their schools' successes or failures.

- *Unions can gather data to improve education and can be sure those data are used wisely.* It is not enough that newspapers publish comparative school data; schools need to be able to use the information to improve. Data have to be available in forms that teachers can use, and they have to be available in forms that the public, media, and politicians are less prone to misuse. Unions that set standards can play a major role in determining how to use the data they reveal.

■ *Unions link the top and the bottom.* Unions are uniquely situated to reconcile the tendency to use testing as a device for micromanagement and the movement toward teacher empowerment as a way to create knowledge-building institutions. By participating in standards-creation, unions can become a powerful voice for improving the tests that are out there and for ensuring that new tests adequately assess student performance.

The Buck Stops Here

At some point America's teachers need to invoke Harry Truman's aphorism and say they will own the problem of standards. It's fine to understand that the problems of schools and teaching are contextual, that our society is deeply unfair, and that the fates are quirky. But context defines the problem; it is not an excuse for not solving it.

Teachers are justified in their position that they can't go it alone. Families and communities have to shoulder responsibility for the conditions children grow up in. Everyone is afraid of being held accountable for that which they can't control, but commitment to quality will make teachers and their unions stronger rather than weaker. The public is much more likely to be tolerant of teachers for organizing around quality improvements, even if progress is difficult, than it is of being offered nostrums.

The NEA's 1994 statement on accountability puts the problem in context and rightly suggests that the entire education community has a stake in quality. But it is silent about what the union will pledge to do unilaterally in pursuit of higher standards. The NEA is a huge organization with a big budget and staff. It can organize a presidential campaign, so why can't it organize for school quality? Rather than the current policy on testing, one would be comforted by a statement such as:

> The NEA pledges to organize around higher student achievement. The NEA will create a system of indicators of school accountability at the national and state levels. It will offer training to its local affiliates in how to gather and interpret indicator data at the local level. It will publish indicator information annually. Where changes in the way teachers work, are trained, or are rewarded will help increase student achievement, the NEA pledges to support those changes.

Conclusion

Teacher unions must take the lead in developing standards for student achievement. When they do, students will benefit from teachers' expertise as mind workers; and unions will become leaders in educational improvement.

GETTING STARTED IN THOUGHT AND ACTION

Thought
- ▶ Get behind the headlines of the debate over standards by reading such books as Marc Tucker and Judy Codding's *Standards for Our Schools*.

Action
- ▶ Examine how your school creates standards by creating different expectations for different groups of students. Consider the effect these differing expectations have on students' experience in school and afterwards.

► Build a culture of achievement rather than aptitude at your school. Begin by turning away from describing students as *smart* or *dumb, talented* or *challenged,* and look instead at whether they attend school regularly, work hard, and complete assignments.

► Form teacher groups to examine student work; create exhibitions of good work.

► Learn how to examine and understand test scores and other kinds of feedback your school gets.

► Negotiate to see that schools get feedback in a timely manner and in a form teachers can use.

5

Evaluating the Work of Peers

ANOTHER WAY unions can link themselves to educational quality is through developing and assuring quality among teachers. Peer review is probably the most powerful demonstration that teachers create and display a knowledge of practice. In the twenty or so school districts that have tried it, teachers have found that peer review brings higher standards to teaching. It significantly changes the conception of teaching work by recognizing the importance of engagement and commitment as well as skill and technique. It recognizes a legitimate role for teachers in establishing and enforcing standards in their own occupation. For unions, it represents both a radical departure from established industrial norms and a rediscovery of traditional craft union and guild functions. Under peer review, the union's role balances protection of individual teachers with protection of teaching.

Both the American Federation of Teachers and the NEA support peer review. And several districts affiliated with each organization have active and successful programs, including Seattle, Washington; Columbus, Ohio; Rochester, New York; and Poway, California.

As it stands now, most teacher assessment is undertaken to meet state mandates or community expectations. Typically, teacher review systems involve short observations of teaching by principals, a checklist of desired characteristics, and some kind of form for recording information. A conference may follow the observations, and teachers typically have the right to comment on a principal's assessment of them.

Peer review is different.

Peer review brings higher standards to teaching. Peer review systems generally have more resources, and thus put forward a more thorough system of evaluation than conventional, administratively driven evaluations. The review plans used in Toledo, Ohio, and Poway, California, for example, assign between ten and twenty novice teachers to each supervising teacher. Assistance and evaluation is the supervisors' full-time job. For new teachers, this intensification means getting more help and a closer look at what expert teachers do.

There is no evidence to support the proposition—perhaps held by peer review's detractors—that teachers would soft-pedal evaluation to save the jobs of their colleagues. In fact, anecdotal evidence suggests peer review is tougher than administrator review. More than administrators, other teachers bear the burden of incompetent colleagues. "To see someone that bad being called a 'teacher' just like I am lowers my stature and self-esteem," said one teacher. Teachers know who's good, and who's not so good. When teachers evaluate other teachers, they are tough and thorough.

Peer review recognizes the importance of engagement and commitment, as well as skill and technique. When supervising teachers spend time with classroom teachers, they are able to consider the teachers' classroom as a whole, rather than isolating details of teacher practice. This enables them to provide a much more useful assessment than a traditional administrative evaluation.

Peer review recognizes a role for teachers in establishing and enforcing standards. Peer review forces teachers to reflect on their craft and define what constitutes good teaching. Where administrative review focuses on accountability—is this teacher good enough?—peer review focuses on learning and growth— how can this teacher improve his or her teaching?

How Peer Review Systems Work

Peer review programs generally operate for novice teachers who have not yet been awarded tenure and for teachers whose performance has deteriorated to the point that disciplinary or dismissal proceedings are imminent.

The idea of peer review is just starting to be applied to ensuring continuous improvement of the majority of experienced teachers. Peer observation, individual growth contracts, and peer mentoring relations are some of the techniques being used. As peer review becomes more commonplace, the connection between peer review and professional development should become stronger. Potentially, unions have a much larger role to play in professional development, including helping teachers prepare for National Board for Professional Teaching Standards certification. Many of the observational and practice-based evaluation techniques developed by the national board can also be applied in peer review.

The twenty or so existing peer review programs vary somewhat in their operation, but generally they are characterized by the following:

■ A governing board of teachers and administrators oversees the whole program. The composition and powers of the board may be referenced in the collective bargaining contract or a memorandum of agreement between the union and district.

- A team of trained teachers coaches and assists the teachers being reviewed and presents evaluative findings to the governing board.

- These "supervising teachers," as they are called in some districts, are generally released from classroom duties, either full- or part-time.

- Generally all novice teachers are assigned to peer review during their probationary period. A supervising teacher is assigned to each new teacher.

- Administrators, teachers, or the teacher union can nominate a poorly performing experienced teacher for intervention by the peer review system. Before deciding to intervene, the governing board determines that there is good cause.

- The governing board hears recommendations from the supervisory teachers, and—based on standards it has developed—it makes continuing employment recommendations to the superintendent and school board. (As is the case in colleges and universities, the school board is the official employer and makes the final decision on employment, but the weight of evidence presented by the peer review governing board almost always determines the decision.)

Conclusion

Organizing around quality and enforcing it with peer review is both radical and traditional. It departs from industrial assumptions about worker protection and the sources of union solidarity. Instead it returns unionism to a more craft-oriented model. The guild and craft traditions, which preceded industrialization, considered workers as members of communities.

It was craft solidarity, not organizing capability, that empowered craft workers. In most craft situations, development and enforcement of standards became part of what unions did and still do.

We believe teachers have little to lose and much to gain from organizing around the quality dimensions of teaching work. Peer review creates an important building block for using unionism as a means to make schools themselves perform better, a subject we address in Part III.

GETTING STARTED IN THOUGHT AND ACTION

Thought

- ▶ Suspend biases about peer review. The practice is mostly controversial in places that don't have it. Give permission to think and examine the evidence.

- ▶ Ask how well the evaluation system now in place promotes and enforces excellence in teaching and assists teachers at all stages in their careers.

- ▶ Read about the developing INTASC (Interstate New Teacher Assistance and Support Consortium) beginning teacher standards; consider how these standards and evaluation methods might be adopted to a peer review system.

- ▶ Read about peer review in action. *United Mind Workers* contains a longer description, and *A Union of Professionals* profiles two peer review districts.

- ▶ Consider what should be the obligation of experienced, expert teachers to set the teaching standards for those entering the district or school.

Action

▶ Negotiate professional development agreements that enhance expertise in coaching and mentoring.

▶ Form a labor-management study group to consider alternatives to the conventional teacher evaluation system for new teachers, those in difficulty, and most importantly, for the larger numbers of teachers who are doing good work but need continually to grow in their careers.

Part III

Organizing Around Transforming Schools

IN *UNITED MIND WORKERS*, we advocate organizing unions around individual schools. Our reasons for this stance have to do with the instability of school districts. Many reform experiments would structurally alter districts. If unions are tied to districts, as they are now, their position will be precarious. Organizing by district could position unions to be left behind, trapped on the wrong side of the gulf opened by historic change. A better strategy is to organize around the smallest feasible unit of organized learning: the school. Schools may look different than they do now, but we think that they will be stable organizational entities for the foreseeable future.

In Part III, we describe a labor-relations system built around relatively autonomous schools. These could be charter schools, schools within a district having substantive site management and governance provisions, or schools in a governance arrangement not yet practiced. Chapter 6 describes what district-level and school-level contracts would look like when they are based on the shared desire for educational achievement. Chapter 7 elaborates on new ways to establish teacher pay, Chapter 8 presents a model for offering teachers stability that is not tied to one specific job, and Chapter 9 offers some ideas for getting started. In Part III, we

- Analyze the shortcomings of current education contracts
- Propose a model for a streamlined, districtwide contract and a detailed school-site compact based on the desire for educational improvement
- Propose models for determining teacher pay and career stability
- Offer concrete steps for embarking on the road to change ▶

6

New Contracting Strategies

FLEXIBILITY, CREATIVITY, the ability to adapt to changing circumstances, and an ethic of continuous improvement are hallmarks of successful modern organizations. As they seek or create opportunities for growth, these organizations are highly responsive to the needs of their customers and clients. Individuals, work teams, and small operating units gain substantial autonomy about how work is to be done and how resources are to be used. Public education has only begun to adopt this organizational spirit.

The evolution of school districts as centralized bureaucracies has created a structure—and an organizational demeanor—that stymies rather than supports change and innovation. School districts tend to function on the command-and-control model, or its only slightly kinder and gentler cousin, monitor-and-compliance. The job of district-level personnel is to ensure that schools hew faithfully to local, state, and federal rules, regulations, and statutes. It is hard to imagine finding a school district that could match the efficiency of a FedEx office, the innovation of a Saturn auto plant, or the entrepreneurial corporate culture of a Hewlett-Packard division.

Teachers' contracts—districtwide agreements between teachers, as represented by their union, and local school boards—developed in response to centralized educational decision making. As power and authority accrued to school-district headquarters, unions also consolidated their efforts, in master contracts, to influence the terms and conditions of employment of those they represented. Viewed in this light, the centralized collective bargaining agreement appears as a rather rational development. Nonetheless, conventional wisdom holds that teachers' contracts are a principal impediment to educational improvement, and we agree—to a point.

Collective bargaining agreements apply a districtwide template to teachers' conditions of employment. The same set of professional rules of engagement applies equally to all teachers in a given school district, regardless of assignment, circumstance, or qualifications. Under the terms of most teachers' contracts, flexibility is discouraged and support for innovation is tepid at best.

In the following section, we describe the current approach to collective bargaining, explain why it's not working, and offer an alternative.

Contracts: The Industrial Model

In collective bargaining as it is currently organized, unions advocate for fair compensation and individual rights for members, but they leave the business of educational policy to school districts. Stated another way, collective bargaining assumes that "bread-and-butter" issues of financial and job security are teachers' concerns, but that the mission of the institution and the content and conduct of the work are not. This approach fails to recognize that teachers are our best mind workers—the people who are best equipped to improve education. Teachers and their unions must reclaim teaching and learning as their concerns.

We propose that the comprehensive districtwide contract be replaced by two new forms of written union-management agreement—a slender district-level contract and a much more encompassing school site educational compact. These agreements would have the effect of recognizing the union as an equal participant in educational improvement, refocusing negotiated agreements on institutional rather than individual welfare, and placing significant educational decision-making authority and responsibility in the hands of schools.

Our Proposal, Part I: Districtwide Contracts

The new central agreement, which would provide a kind of bare-bones philosophical and operational architecture, would be structured around educational goals toward which all schools would strive. The document would also contain a few basic wage and working condition provisions, many of which could be subject to school-site modification. More comprehensive agreements would be forged at local schools.

The new central agreement we propose has six provisions:

1 *Unions and management would share joint responsibility for educational improvement.* The goal for both groups would be to improve student achievement.

2 *Salaries and benefits would be calculated to reward teacher achievement and allow for teacher flexibility.* Pay would be based on teachers' demonstrated knowledge and skills, rather than exclusively on longevity and accumulated course credit, as they are now. Benefits would not belong to the individual district, but would instead be independent and portable, making it easier for teachers to pursue professional opportunities. (Chapter 7 looks at salary setting in greater detail.)

3 *Professional development would be school-based, rather than district-based.* In a system that places high value on flexibility, innovation, and entrepreneurship, professional development would enable employees to continuously adapt to new and often unanticipated circumstances.

4 *Rather than specifying a rigid school year calendar, the new districtwide contract would establish instructional time minimums.* This would allow for school flexibility, with the aim of increasing student achievement, not necessarily time in the classroom.

5 *Agreements would ensure organizational security for the union and employment security for teachers.* The contract would acknowledge the union as the sole supplier of teachers, and all teachers would be required to pay fees to the union. Teachers would be guaranteed *employment* security—the right to a teaching position in the district—but not necessarily *job* security guaranteeing them a particular job at a particular school. Teachers' positions would depend on schools' needs.

6 *Dispute resolution would focus on preserving the integrity of the educational institution and the goals it is attempting to achieve.* This new formulation would attempt to balance institutional welfare—ensuring the district and its schools can achieve their educational goals—with individual rights— ensuring that the system does not treat individual teachers in an arbitrary or capricious manner.

Our Proposal, Part II: School-Based Compacts

The new districtwide contract frames the basics. The real power of the system, however, lies in allowing the heart of the educational enterprise to be shaped by the people who must make it work—the ones at the school site.

We call the school's contract a *compact.* The agreement would be developed at individual schools by the administrators, teachers, and support staff who work there. Rather than serving as an enumeration of accrued employment rights, the educational compact would represent a social contract between the school and its community.

The system we propose here confronts the challenges of many school-based management operations. Critical education decisions—such as hiring and evaluation of personnel, curriculum and instruction, and allocation of the majority of the school's operating resources—would become the province of schools through their educational compacts. Moreover, schools would be held responsible for the results of their actions. Accountability would be assessed against the district's and the school's measurable educational goals, and rewards and consequences would flow accordingly.

There are eight components to the compact we propose:

1 *Philosophy and Student Performance Targets:* The school staff and community would reach consensus on the answer to the question: What does our school stand for? In doing so, they would determine the school's operating mission and principles.

2 *Resource Allocation:* With 90 percent of funds controlled at the school site—each school's funding would be determined on a per-pupil basis—parties to the school compact would establish procedures by which to determine resource allocation priorities.

3 *Hiring:* Hiring would take place at the school site, with each school making decisions about the composition of its staff.

The union would send qualified applicants to the school, but would not take part in hiring decisions.

4 *Salary Decisions:* While the district contract would set salaries based on demonstrated knowledge and skill, individual schools could decide to offer signing incentives to well-suited teachers, or bonuses to teachers who have made a special contribution.

5 *Class and Course Organization:* Each school would make decisions about such issues as the number of school days in the year (within the minimums set by the district), the length of class periods, class size, and whether or when to team-teach. Enhancing students' education would be the ultimate goal of these organizational decisions.

6 *Professional Development and Professional Performance:* Each school would determine its professional development program tied specifically to increasing teachers' capacity to improve student educational performance. The compact, for example, might reward teachers who become certified through the National Board for Professional Teaching Standards.

7 *Quality Assurance and Community Support:* Teachers would agree to guarantee the quality of the educational program; in exchange, parents and community members would commit to support teachers and the school.

8 *Dispute Resolution:* The first step of a dispute resolution mechanism would involve an informal meeting among the parties involved to try to resolve the problem. If that failed, the issue would be submitted to a school-based panel that would act as a kind of umpire, taking both the school's welfare and the individuals' rights into account.

Conclusion

School districts are no longer secure entities around which to organize. Instead we propose that only the bare bones of union agreements be made at the district level, with most contractual issues being decided at each school site. Site-based agreements allow teachers and teacher unions to keep their eyes on the prize: educational improvement.

GETTING STARTED IN THOUGHT AND ACTION

Thought

▶ Study schools that successfully operate with substantial autonomy: schools with strong site decision systems. Learn the implications for local unions from how these schools work.

▶ Look at different forms of labor contracts. *A Union of Professionals* profiles several districts, including Glenview, Illinois, that have crafted unusual agreements. Also, Barry and Irving Bluestone's *Negotiating the Future* provides examples of labor compacts in industry.

Action

▶ Form a union committee to begin to think through what a school-level agreement would look like. How would it be structured? How would it be implemented? What kind of training would people need to make it work?

▶ Be sensitive to the time demands of reform. Autonomous schools empower teachers, but also fatigue them. Make thoughtful decisions about activities that waste time and activities that schools do now that could be suspended.

▶ Train staff and members in how to understand a school budget, a necessary precursor to developing site-based compacts.

7

Hiring and Rewarding Teachers

UNDER A RESULTS-BASED education model, schools need teachers who can best contribute to the school's educational goals and objectives. As proposed in our new labor agreements, central districts would no longer be responsible for hiring and assigning teachers. Instead, local schools would have authority for all staffing decisions. Hiring criteria and procedures would be outlined in the school-based compact (and local teachers would have a role in this process). Salaries would be based on the district's baseline salary schedule, but schools would be free, within the limits of their available resources, to offer additional financial compensation in order to attract teachers with particular knowledge and skills.

Paying for Knowledge and Skills

Compensation for nearly all the nation's five million teachers is currently structured around the "standard single salary schedule." This unified salary structure was instituted to achieve equitable treatment of male and female teachers and to prevent political and professional favoritism. Under this system, teachers advance vertically by virtue of longevity in the district, and horizontally with accrued course credit.

In our view, this uniform salary structure is a mismatch with the standards-based education system envisioned under our new union model. Schools that aim for high performance rely highly on a teacher's innovative spirit and professional expertise—and require a new way of rewarding such teachers. We propose instituting a salary schedule that would be based on demonstrated knowledge and skill. Under this new system, as proposed by Allan Odden, Carolyn Kelley, and others, teachers would continue to be paid based on their years of service but would be entitled to added compensation for acquiring new skills and expertise and for assuming new roles and responsibilities. Teacher skills might be described as follows:

- *Depth skills:* Expertise in particular functional or disciplinary areas—in teaching itself or in particular subjects
- *Breadth skills*: Expertise in areas such as curriculum development, counseling, and professional development
- *Vertical skills*: Expertise in school management, planning, and leadership areas

Advantages of Skill-Based Pay Systems

Unlike merit pay systems, which can breed favoritism and individual competitiveness among teachers—and destroy the teamwork and cooperation so necessary for school improvement—skill-based pay systems can be fairer and more equitable. They offer the following advantages:

- They more accurately reflect the teacher's professional contribution and commitment to the school's educational goals and objectives.
- They can be awarded equally to all teachers who demonstrate the requisite skills.
- They enable teachers to be rewarded for accomplishment without causing undue professional competition.

■ They offer teachers an incentive to grow professionally and to remain in teaching.

Conclusion: The Union's Role

Under our new collective bargaining approach, the district—and the union—would jointly agree on the teaching skills required to receive higher compensation (such as certification through the National Board for Professional Teaching Standards) and the method for assessing these skills. The basic salary schedule and skill incentives would ultimately be based on the joint union-management assessment of the district's goals and needs.

Once the salary structures and skill incentives are established, the ongoing governance of the system would fall to a joint union-management salary board. This board would be responsible for ensuring that salaries remain appropriately competitive, that fair processes are used in judging a teacher's skill development, and that new skills acquired are adequately compensated.

GETTING STARTED IN THOUGHT AND ACTION

Thought

▶ Study alternatives to the current salary schedules: those that pay for knowledge and skill rather than credit hours earned. Read such books as Allan Odden and Carolyn Kelley's *Paying Teachers for What They Know and Do.*

Action

▶ Negotiate a contract item to establish a joint union-management team to study salary scale alternatives and make recommendations for the next—*not the current*—contract.

8

Creating More Career Flexibility for Teachers

FROM THE DAYS of the guilds forward, unions have served as market intermediaries, protecting their members' economic and social interests. Craftworker and artisan unions, guilds, and professional associations also protect the market by keeping out shoddy goods, bad services, and incompetent persons. Unions thus become part of the market solution to obtaining an adequate supply of qualified workers: the visible fingers of the unseen hand.

Historically, teachers and most other twentieth-century workers gained economic security by a set of rights attached to their jobs. Tenure and seniority were the major keys to security. But this relationship is beginning to break down as schools operate with:

- Part-time employees who are part of the organization, but not entirely so

- Contractual workers who perform vital functions but are not on the payroll

- Consultants who perform highly strategic activities but only for a short period of time

- Volunteers or other community members who render valuable service, but who may never have an economic relationship to the school

Schools as job sites have become highly organic entities that change rapidly with conditions. In this setting, employment is likely to be fluid. As a result, the union's historical weapon of building a set of rights around a particular job is challenged, leaving the union with two possible avenues of action. One is to fight at each of the boundaries: redefinition of teacher work, contracting out, the use of interns, substitution of volunteers or employees of other organizations and agencies. The other is for the union to begin to organize around career security rather than job security.

Thus we must ask, what is a "good teaching job" if it is not necessarily anchored in a single workplace? What would have to be the characteristics of teaching work that would attract talented people to teaching and evoke from them high levels of dedication, caring, and productivity? We believe the evidence favors a labor market that allows teachers to enter and leave as need be, one that allows teachers to recharge their intellects and their psyches, yet one that allows teachers a good measure of financial security through whatever transitions their career development—and student improvement—require.

What might such a system look like?

We believe that teachers would like to shape their jobs with individual preferences about the intensity and duration of their work. One of teaching's attractions has been that it allows a reasonably healthy balance among workplace, family, and community obligations. In the past, the relatively short on-campus day and school year made teaching a welcoming occupation to mothers with children. Now, with school work intensifying and teachers' roles and responsibilities increasing, both male and female teachers are looking for ways to create balance in their lives. While other professions have approached the question of balance either with superhuman expectations or with separate "mommy" or "daddy" tracks, teaching could be constructed to allow workers to increase or decrease the intensity of their work.

We believe teachers would be attracted by the prospect of creating a professional practice, identifying themselves as teachers rather than as civil servants. Bureaucratic job definitions don't allow for a great deal of self-expression. Even the master and mentor teacher plans that have been developed over the last decade seem sterile alongside the kinds of interesting projects teachers develop for themselves.

It may well be that some teachers would choose a practice centered on creating curriculum or developing educational software. Any specific school might have need of such a person only for an intense period lasting a few months, so movement from place to place would be a normal part of such a person's practice. Other teachers would find high levels of identification with particular towns or communities, and thus would want to stay in the same physical location, but they might want to change areas of teaching or move from full-time teaching to counseling or developing a new program. Such teachers would need both the stability of a school and the freedom of change.

We believe that teachers want the ability to be proactive in the face of adversity. Currently, when bad things happen at school, teachers hunker down. They can engage in trench warfare with a bad principal and suffer through a place that they know has lost its spirit and academic integrity, but they rarely have an effective exit option. The system is set up to keep people in. The experience of waitress unions offers an alternative system in which a union helps employees move from unworkable situations to better ones. If a boss or headwaiter was abusive and dictatorial, the waitress sought work elsewhere, and eventually that establishment had difficulty hiring qualified people. The idea of assigning people to work in places they didn't want to go disappeared, and many debilitating workplace grievances were relieved by separating the combatants .

Gaining career flexibility means structuring teaching work in different ways. These are big changes, and for some unions and school districts they may lie in the future. In others, particularly in locations experimenting with large-scale charter school movements, the need to structure teaching careers differently may be more immediate. In *United Mind Workers,* we introduce several new structures that promote career flexibility.

- *The electronic hiring hall:* Under this model, unions provide schools with qualified applicants for vacant positions, and provide teachers with union security, job placement and counseling services, and access to training and development.

- *A career ladder with teaching at the top:* Most ideas about a teaching career begin with teaching at the bottom of a career ladder and build up from there. We suggest a different ladder, one that places classroom teaching at the top and creates an orderly career progression into teaching. This would create a situation in which seasoned teachers could train and socialize new entrants and ensure their quality.

- *Portable pensions and benefits:* Localized pensions and benefits create rigidity in the teacher labor market. Unions should serve as the plan holder for health care and other benefits, allowing teachers the kind of flexibility they need both to pursue their professional goals, and to balance career and family responsibilities. With portable benefits, teachers can move between jobs and districts without penalty.

- *Redefining tenure:* We support the notion that teachers with seniority should accrue employment security; however, we believe that when that security is tied to a specific job at a specific site, a school's ability to meet the changing needs of its students is hampered. We suggest, instead, that employment security be guaranteed through the hiring hall, with teachers guaranteed employment, but not necessarily the same job at the same school.

- *Encouraging teachers to own their profession:* Teachers need ownership, not only of specific initiatives at their schools, but of their craft, and the intellectual property involved. Unions can help in two ways: first, by allowing teachers more voice in creating their schools than the current bureaucracy allows; and second, by helping teachers gain distinction and recognition as teachers.

Conclusion

Organizing teaching around career security rather than job security anticipates a decline in bureaucratic employment and a rise in more varied work arrangements in which job definitions change frequently and the freedom to move from one job or location to another is prized. It makes sense for unions to anticipate these changes, redefine their role, and find ways to gain legitimacy with workers in a dynamic and knowledge-intensive society.

GETTING STARTED IN THOUGHT AND ACTION

Thought

▶ Explore examples of career ladders that promote para-professionals, interns, and other staff who are not fully credentialed.

▶ Read recent NEA research on different pension systems.

▶ Within your local union, consider what an appropriate career ladder for your district would look like.

Action

▶ Actively promote pension and benefit portability in state and national organizations.

▶ Set up a state task force to study models of teacher ownership of schools.

9

What Teachers Can Do Now

REORGANIZING TEACHERS as knowledge workers rather than industrial workers is a daunting task that requires changing some of the most fundamental aspects of public education as we know it. But it is also a do-able task, one that allows local teacher unions to undertake pieces of the challenge as their own, as some already have. Although some of the changes called for in *United Mind Workers* require legislation and other public policy intervention, much can be accomplished incrementally within schools and districts.

Talking with Teachers

Teachers' sense of their work is tied to the jobs they know and know how to do. Profound changes in those jobs are very threatening, to teachers, and to their unions. But change is not optional; the new economy and the new instructional core will change teaching. Teachers can get involved in the process by

- Reading books about the coming changes
- Learning more about their students' families and the changes they have undergone
- Using this booklet as the basis for discussion and action

Professional Development and Peer Review

Peer review is a natural outgrowth of professional development, a claim about expertise. If teacher unions demonstrate their capacity to enhance educational quality through peer review, little can stand in their way. Organized teachers would gain unbeatable influence by saying:

- We will take joint custody of reform.
- We will evaluate ourselves and hold ourselves to high, and public, professional standards.
- We will come to understand our students' lives and advocate for them before we advocate for ourselves.

Making Schools Smarter

Once teachers start to organize around their own practice, they gain a vision of how schools need to be organized. School reorganization then becomes an exercise in building a learning community, rather than simply dividing up managerial responsibility. Teachers become the experts in school change, and union employees become facilitators of that process.

Organizing Parents

Parents can be powerful allies, rather than the "enemy within," and unions have substantive services to offer them—both advocacy and support in raising their families. There are two paths for gaining parent and public support for the educational labor market we envision:

- First, do everything possible to convince parents that teachers and teacher unions are on their side, that they support things that parents want done, and that they can communicate directly with parents.

■ Second, create a classification of membership for parents or form partnerships with parent-based organizations. Teacher unions can help parents in the tough job of child-rearing by, for example, developing educational aids and offering guidance on how to help their children with homework and emotional issues.

Conclusion

Teachers and teacher unions need to begin the process of change now, rather than being swept along by currents too strong to resist. The more they do now, the more say they will have in determining what the institution of education will look like in the knowledge era. And no one is better qualified to take the lead in shaping the future.

Organizing the Other Half of Teaching

TEACHER UNIONS were formed through one of the most successful worker organizing campaigns in history. In little more than twenty years, U.S. teachers moved from being "spoken for" by school administrators to representing their own economic interests. The next struggle for teacher unions is organizing "the other half of teaching"—representing teachers as educators. By this we mean supporting the skill and dedication that individual union members apply every day to their work in their classrooms and advocating for the teaching profession as a whole.

This new unionizing task promises to be a tough job because public education itself is changing, and the occupation of teaching is evolving so rapidly. It will involve rethinking labor law so that unions can better advocate not only for the kinds of jobs that teachers currently have, but for the kinds of careers that teachers may have in the future.

This task also offers a great opportunity. For the first time, it gives unions and teachers a substantive leadership role in improving the quality of America's schools and in transforming the very institution of education.

If unions can effectively advocate for children and can succeed in telling their stories, they can succeed in re-creating a politics of justice, tolerance, and kindness. It is work worth doing.

Resources

Bluestone, B., and Bluestone, I. *Negotiating the Future: A Labor Perspective on American Business.* New York: Basic Books, 1992.

Darling-Hammond, L. *The Right to Learn: A Blueprint for Creating Schools That Work.* San Francisco: Jossey-Bass, 1997.

Heckscher, C. *White-Collar Blues: Management Loyalties in an Age of Corporate Restructuring.* New York: Basic Books, 1995.

Johnson, S. M. *Teachers at Work: Achieving Success in Our Schools.* New York: Basic Books, 1990.

Kerchner, C. T., and Koppich, J. E. *A Union of Professionals: Unions and Management in Turbulent Times.* New York: Teacher's College Press, 1993.

Kerchner, C. T., Koppich, J. E., and Weeres, J. C. *United Mind Workers: Unions and Teaching in the Knowledge Society.* San Francisco: Jossey-Bass, 1997.

Meier, D. *The Power of Their Ideas: Lessons for America from a Small School in Harlem.* Boston: Beacon Press, 1995.

Murnane, R. J., and Levy, F. *Teaching the New Basic Skills: Principles for Educating Children to Thrive in a Changing Economy.* New York: Free Press, 1996.

Odden, A., and Kelley, C. *Paying Teachers for What They Know and Do.* Thousand Oaks, Calif.: Corwin Press, 1997.

Reich, R. B. *The Work of Nations: Preparing Ourselves for 21st Century Capitalism.* New York: Knopf, 1991.

Tucker, M. S., and Codding, J. B. *Standards for Our Schools: How to Set Them, Measure Them, and Reach Them.* San Francisco: Jossey-Bass, 1998.

Wilson, W. J. *When Work Disappears: The World of the New Urban Poor.* New York: Alfred A. Knopf.

Organizations

AFL-CIO
815 16th Street, NW
Washington, DC 20036
(202) 637–5000
(202) 637–5058 fax
www.aflcio.org

American Federation of Teachers
555 New Jersey Avenue
Washington, DC 20079
(202) 879–4400
www.aft.org

Education Week
4301 Connecticut Avenue, Suite 250
Washington, DC 20008
(202) 364–4114
www.edweek.org

National Board for Professional
  Teaching Standards
2655 Evergreen Road, Suite 400
Southfield, MI 48076
(800) 229–9074
(248) 351–4444
www.nbpts.org

National Commission on Teaching and
  America's Future (NCTAF)
Teachers College, Columbia University
525 West 120th Street
110 Main Hall (Box 117)
New York, NY 10027
(888) 492–1241
(212) 678–4142
www.tc.columbia.edu/~teachcomm

To order NCTAF publications, contact:
  Kutztown Publishing Co., Inc.
  15076 Kutztown Road
  Kutztown, PA 19530–0326
  (888) 492–1241
  fax: (610) 683–5616

National Education Association
1201 16th Street, NW
Washington, DC 20036–3290
(202) 833–4000
www.nea.org

Teacher Union Reform Network
Adam Urbanski, director
c/o Rochester Teachers Union
30 North Union Street, Suite 301
Rochester, NY 14607
(716) 546–2681
www.gse.ucla.edu/turn/turn.html

The Authors

CHARLES TAYLOR KERCHNER is Hollis P. Allen professor of education at Claremont Graduate University in Claremont, California. He is coauthor of *United Mind Workers: Unions and Teaching in the Knowledge Society, A Union of Professionals,* and *The Changing Idea of a Teachers' Union.* E-mail: Charles.Kerchner@cgu.edu.

JULIA E. KOPPICH is president of Julia E. Koppich and Associates, a San Francisco–based education consulting firm. She and Kerchner are the authors of *A Union of Professionals,* and she is coauthor of *United Mind Workers.* E-mail: JKoppich@sirius.com.

JOSEPH G. WEERES is professor of education at Claremont Graduate School and a coauthor of *United Mind Workers.* He is also coauthor of *Voices from the Inside: A Report on Schooling from Inside the Classroom.* E-mail: Joseph.Weeres@cgu.edu.

Keeping Up-to-Date

The authors have established *United Mind Workers* web pages that contain portions of the book, research reports, and work in progress as well as links to other labor and teacher reform web pages and links to the authors' electronic mail boxes. For the web pages, go to: www.cgu.edu. Then click on FACULTY, then Kerchner.

9 780787 943349